What a Great Question!

Your Roadmap to Meaningful Relationships
and Impactful Leadership

By

Terry-Lyn Stevens

Author: Terry-Lyn Stevens

Title: What a great question! Your Roadmap to Meaningful Relationships and Impactful Leadership

ISBN: 979-8-89269-122-2

Subjects: Coaching | Communication | Leadership | Management

https://www.terry-lyn.com.au/

Table of Contents

About the author

Terry-Lyn is a leadership development specialist and executive coach.

She offers a boutique consulting service for businesses and individuals looking to advance their people, performance and workplace culture.

Since 2002 she's worked alongside corporates and SMEs to grow leadership capabilities and thriving cultures. Her approach is simple, customised and real.

She provides facilitation, training and coaching programs that make a genuine difference to the financial performance of businesses and the individuals within them.

Terry-Lyn believes that as humans, we need to grow. It's healthy for our minds and wellbeing.

"Our mindset matters. I've often wondered why some of us shy away from change and growth. It can be empowering. It helps us thrive. We all have the right to flourish. What holds you back?"

How to use this book

Congratulations on choosing "What a Great Question" as your companion on your journey of self-discovery and personal growth.

To make the most of this book, consider the following tips:

Set Aside Dedicated Time
Carve out a few minutes each day or week to engage with the questions in this book. Creating a routine will help you establish a habit of introspection and reflection.

Create a Comfortable Space
Find a quiet, comfortable space where you can focus without distractions. Whether it's a cosy corner of your home or a tranquil outdoor spot, the right environment can enhance your reflective practice.

Journal Your Responses
Use this book, or a notebook or journal to record your thoughts and answers to the questions. Writing down your responses adds a level of commitment to the process and allows you to revisit your insights later.

Be Honest and Open

There are no right or wrong answers to the questions in this book. Be honest with yourself, even if the answers are uncomfortable or challenging. True growth often comes from facing difficult truths.

Embrace Curiosity

Approach each question with curiosity and an open mind. Allow yourself to explore new ideas and perspectives. You might be surprised by the insights you uncover.

Use the Book Flexibly

While you can certainly work through the questions in order, feel free to jump around the book based on what resonates with you at any given moment. Some questions may be more relevant at certain times in your life than others.

Share and Discuss

If you feel comfortable, share your reflections and insights with a trusted friend or family member. Engaging in meaningful conversations about the questions can deepen your understanding and strengthen your relationships.

Set Goals and Take Action

As you reflect on your responses, consider how they can inform your actions and decisions. Use the insights gained from this book to set goals and take concrete steps toward a more fulfilling life.

Practice Patience and Self-Compassion
Self-discovery is a lifelong journey, and it's okay to not have all
the answers immediately. Be patient with yourself and practice
self-compassion along the way.

Revisit and Reflect
Periodically revisit your journal entries and reflect on how your
answers have evolved over time. This book can serve as a
valuable tool for tracking your personal growth and progress.

Remember that "What a Great Question" is a tool designed to
help you unlock your inner wisdom and navigate life's
complexities with greater clarity and purpose.

Your unique journey of self-discovery awaits, and these
questions are your guides. Embrace them with an open heart
and mind, and you'll uncover the incredible depth of insight
and potential within you. Enjoy the adventure!

Take time to reflect,

01

Journey to Self-Discovery and Personal Development

In the journey of self-discovery and personal development, we embark on a profound exploration of ourselves—our values, strengths, weaknesses, and aspirations.

These questions are a doorway to the heart of who we are and who we aspire to become. By asking the right questions and delving into our innermost thoughts and feelings, we unlock the potential for growth and transformation.

The power of self-awareness is immense, and within these pages, you will find ten questions designed to guide you on this introspective voyage.

Each question carries with it the promise of insight, clarity, and the opportunity to take meaningful steps towards your personal development goals.

As you journal your responses, you'll uncover the path to a more authenti fulfilled

What are your core values, and how do they guide your life?

Values are the 'rudder of the ship' they give direction and guidance to what is important to you . When aligned and congruent, things come with ease.

This question helps you understand what truly matters to you.

Action: Reflect on your values and align your actions with them for a more fulfilling life.

What are your strengths, and how can you leverage them?

Knowing your unique strengths gives you a better understanding of
yourself and how you best operate.
Recognising your strengths boosts self-confidence.

Action: Focus on using your strengths in your daily activities and
pursuits.

What limiting beliefs hold you back, and how can you challenge them?

Limiting beliefs are a thought or a state of mind that you think is an absolute truth and stops you from doing certain things. Identifying limiting beliefs leads to personal growth.

Action: Work on changing negative thought patterns to achieve your goals.

What experiences have shaped your identity the most?

Understanding your past helps you make informed decisions. Our past failures teach us resilience, perseverance and the importance of adapting to changing circumstances. They help us be a better version of ourselves.

Action: Use insights from your past to set future intentions.

What are your short-term and long-term personal goals?

The future depends on what you do today. Setting clear goals provides direction, motivation and belief within yourself.
Writing down and sharing your goals with a friend, increases achievement thinking.

Action: Break down your goals into actionable steps and track your progress.

What habits contribute positively to your well-being?

Identifying positive habits will enhance your quality of life, they allow you to take back control and become the architect of your life.

Action: Cultivate and reinforce these habits in your daily routine.

What brings you joy and fulfillment in life?

Recognising sources of happiness will give you longevity and a more satisfying life.

Action: Prioritise activities and relationships that bring you joy.

What role does self-care play in your life, and how can you improve it?

Practising self-care on a regular basis, maintains mental and emotional health. Small acts for a ripple effect.

Action: Develop a self-care routine and stick to it consistently.

What are your most significant fears, and how can you overcome them?

Acknowledging your fears will help you understand what you are feeling and allow you to work overcoming them.
Confronting fears leads to personal growth and resilience.

Action: Take small steps to face your fears and build confidence.

How do you define success, and are you currently on the right path to achieve it?

Clarifying your definition of success and visualising this, helps you stay focused, align your actions and goals to what matters to you.

Action: Regularly evaluate your progress and adjust your path as needed.

02

Communication and Interpersonal Relationships

Human connection is the essence of our existence, and the quality of our relationships hinges on effective communication.

This section delves into the art of communication and the intricacies of interpersonal dynamics.

By asking thoughtful questions and examining the way we interact with others, we can nurture deeper connections, resolve conflicts, and build bonds that last a lifetime.

These ten questions are your companions on the journey to becoming a better communicator and forging stronger, more meaningful relationships.

As you ponder these inquiries and record your thoughts, you'll gain valuable insights into your communication style, learn to navigate social complexities, and ultimately enhance the way you connect with those around

What are your communication strengths and limitations?

Knowing and adapting your communication style can help you overcome diversities, build trust and create conditions for having improved relationships.

Action: Work on enhancing your strengths and addressing weaknesses.

What active listening skills can you develop to improve your relationships?

Active listeners keeps you engaged in a conversation in a positive way. It helps foster better awareness, understanding and empathy for self and others.

Action: Practice attentive listening in conversations with others.

How do you handle conflicts, and can you improve your conflict resolution skills?

Effective conflict resolution strengthens relationships, it increases your understanding of the other person, builds trust and aligns you to being the person you want to be.

Action: Learn conflict resolution techniques and practice them.

What non-verbal cues do you send, and how do they affect your interactions?

You nonverbal communication cues with the way you listen, look, move and react communicates whether you care or not. And impact the message you want to convey. Being consciously aware of your non-verbal cues can impact the message you convey.

Action: Be mindful of your body language and facial expressions.

What are your boundaries in relationships, and how can you communicate them?

Setting and communicating boundaries is essential for healthy relationships and to protect our values that are important to us.

Action: Clearly express your boundaries and respect those of others.

Who are the people who uplift you and bring positivity into your life?

Identifying positive influences helps nurture meaningful relationships, and challenges you to become a better version of yourself.

Action: Spend more time with those who uplift and support you.

How do you express gratitude and appreciation to those around you?

Expressing gratitude strengthens bonds and fosters positivity, it reduces negativity, builds a foundation of trust and fulfilling relationships.

Action: Regularly show appreciation to the people in your life.

What is your communication goal in a specific relationship, and how can you achieve it?

Setting communication goals improves the quality of interactions, helps you voice your opinions and gives clarity.

Action: Communicate openly and work toward your relationship goals.

What role does empathy play in your relationships, and how can you enhance it?

Empathy promotes understanding and connection, with yourself and others.

Action: Practice putting yourself in others' shoes and genuinely understanding their perspective.

How can you build trust in your relationships, and what steps can you take to rebuild trust if it's been damaged?

Trust is the foundation of healthy relationships, it increases closeness and safety.

Action: Consistently demonstrate trustworthiness and take proactive steps to rebuild trust when necessary.

03

Goal Setting and Planning

Setting goals is the compass that guides us through life's myriad possibilities, helping us navigate the vast sea of opportunities and challenges.

In this section, we embark on a journey of purposeful goal setting and strategic planning. Each question in this chapter serves as a guiding star, illuminating the path to your dreams and ambitions.

By examining your aspirations, breaking them down into actionable steps, and strategising for success, you'll harness the power of intention to shape your future.

These ten questions are the foundation upon which you'll construct your goals, and through journaling your responses, you'll transform aspirations into achievements, and dreams into reality.

Whether you seek personal or professional growth, these questions will equip you with the tools you need to set your course and navigate the journey ahead.

What are your most important life goals, and why are they meaningful to you?

Identifying meaningful goals provides motivation and purpose, it allows us to create a vision of how we would like our life to be.

Action: Break down your goals into smaller, actionable steps.

What obstacles might you encounter while pursuing your goals, and how can you overcome them?

Recognising potential challenges allows for better preparation. Without adversity, we would not grow or learn, or have opportunity to develop our resilience.

Action: Develop strategies to address obstacles as they arise.

How do you prioritise your goals, and are you allocating your resources effectively?

Effective prioritisation will minimize stress, save time and ensures you focus on what matters most.

Action: Use time management techniques to allocate resources wisely.

What short-term goals can you set to make progress toward your long-term aspirations?

Short-term goals provide a roadmap to long-term success, it embeds you feeling you have achieved this builds self esteem and motivation to continue.

Action: Break down long-term goals into smaller, achievable milestones.

What is your plan for maintaining motivation and resilience during setbacks?

Taking initiative helps with motivation and resilience and are key to achieving goals.

Action: Create a support system and practice self-care to stay motivated.

How do you measure success in relation to your goals, and when do you know you've achieved them?

Clear success criteria help track progress, it gives you the feeling of excitement and getting closer to your goal.

Action: Set specific, measurable goals with defined success indicators.

What new skills or knowledge do you need to acquire to reach your goals, and how will you acquire them?

Continuous learning enhances goal attainment, expands skills and builds a growth mindset.

Action: Identify learning resources and commit to ongoing education.

Who can you collaborate with to help you achieve your goals, and how can you build those relationships?

Collaboration can accelerate progress and provide support. It helps eliminate the need to face things on your own.

Action: Network and nurture relationships with potential collaborators.

How do you adapt your goals when circumstances change, and how do you stay flexible in your approach?

Adaptability is essential in achieving evolving goals.

Action: Regularly review and adjust your goals as needed.

What is your plan for celebrating your achievements along the way?

Celebrating milestones reinforces motivation, it creates positive associations with learning and builds self-esteem and growth.

Action: Set up rewards and celebrations for reaching goals and milestones.

04

Feedback and Improvement

Feedback is the compass that guides our journey of self-improvement and growth.

It is the mirror that reflects our strengths and weaknesses, the catalyst for change, and the key to achieving our highest potential.

This section delves into the art of feedback—how to give it, receive it, and leverage it for personal and professional development.

The ten questions within these pages will encourage you to embrace feedback as a gift, to learn from both success and failure, and to continually refine your skills and knowledge.

Through thoughtful reflection and journaling, you'll unlock the secrets to becoming the best version of yourself and foster a culture of continuous improvement in every aspect of your life.

How open are you to receiving feedback, and what is your initial reaction when you receive criticism?

Embracing feedback is essential for personal growth.

Action: Practice active listening and consider feedback as an opportunity for improvement.

What specific feedback have you received in the past that has helped you grow, and how have you applied it?

Learning from past feedback enhances self-awareness and recognise your patterns to avoid repeating mistakes.

Action: Reflect on previous feedback and make positive changes.

How do you provide constructive feedback to others, and what steps can you take to improve your feedback skills?

Effective feedback fosters growth in others and strengthens relationships.

Action: Develop a feedback framework and practice delivering feedback constructively.

What self-assessment tools or methods do you use to evaluate your performance and progress?

Self-assessment enhances self-awareness and improvement.

Action: Incorporate self-assessment into your regular routine.

How do you handle failure, and what strategies can you employ to turn setbacks into opportunities for growth?

Learning from failure is essential for personal development. Look at what is its positive intention for you.

Action: Analyse failures, extract lessons, and adjust your approach.

What are your long-term improvement goals, and how can you track your progress toward them?

Setting improvement goals guides your personal growth journey and builds on achievement thinking.

Action: Create a plan with measurable milestones to monitor progress.

Who are your mentors or role models, and how can their experiences inspire your own growth?

Learning from others' experiences accelerates confidence and personal development.

Action: Seek guidance and insights from mentors and role models.

What habits or behaviours do you want to change or eliminate, and what strategies can you employ to do so?

Breaking negative habits that no longer align with you is crucial for personal improvement.

Action: Identify triggers, create replacement habits, and track your progress.

How do you seek out new opportunities for learning and growth in your personal and professional life?

Continual learning and growth lead to a fulfilling life.

Action: Be proactive in seeking out learning experiences and challenges.

What is your strategy for maintaining a growth mindset, and how do you stay motivated to improve yourself continually?

A growth mindset fuels personal development and resilience.

Action: Embrace challenges, view failures as opportunities, and stay committed to lifelong learning.

05

Leadership and Power Dynamics

Leadership is not merely a position; it is an art, a responsibility, and a journey of influence.

This chapter explores the multifaceted world of leadership and the intricate dynamics of power.

Whether you are a seasoned leader or aspiring to lead, these ten questions will help you refine your leadership style, build trust, and navigate the complexities of leading teams and organizations.

Through self-examination, strategic thinking, and a commitment to ethical leadership, you'll develop the skills and insights needed to make a positive impact in your sphere of influence.

As you engage with these questions and journal your responses, you'll embark on a transformative leadership journey that leaves a lasting legacy of positive change.

What kind of leader do you aspire to be, and what values will guide your leadership?

Defining your leadership style is the foundation for effective leadership.

Action: Align your actions with your leadership values and continually refine your approach.

How do you build trust and credibility as a leader, and what steps can you take to maintain them?

Trust is essential for effective leadership.

Action: Lead with integrity, consistency, and transparency.

How do you handle power and authority, and what safeguards can you put in place to prevent misuse of power?

Responsible power management is critical for ethical leadership.

Action: Establish checks and balances to ensure power is used responsibly.

What strategies can you employ to inspire, motivate and influence your team effectively?

Motivated teams are more productive, loyal, and committed to achieving the best outcomes.

Action: Tailor your leadership style to the needs and aspirations of your team members.

How do you handle conflicts and disagreements within your team, and how can you turn them into opportunities for growth?

Effective conflict resolution strengthens team dynamics.

Action: Create a safe space for open communication and collaborative problem-solving.

What is your plan for developing the leadership skills of those you lead, and how can you empower them to grow?

Developing others promotes a culture of continuous improvement.

Action: Provide mentorship, training, and opportunities for skill development.

How do you lead by example, and how can you ensure your actions align with your leadership values?

Leading by example fosters respect and trust.

Action: Continually assess your actions and their alignment with your leadership values.

What strategies can you use to navigate complex power dynamics in your organisation or community?

Understanding power dynamics is crucial for effective leadership.

Action: Build alliances, gather information, and stay adaptable in complex situations.

How do you handle criticism and feedback as a leader, and how can you use it to improve your leadership skills?

Feedback is valuable for leadership growth.

Action: Actively seek feedback from team members and take constructive steps to improve.

What legacy do you want to leave as a leader, and how can you work toward it throughout your leadership journey?

A leader's legacy is a testament to their lasting impact on individuals and organisations.

Action: Continually align your actions with your desired legacy, mentor and inspire those around you, and consistently embody the values and principles you wish to pass on to future leaders.

Closing Thoughts

In the pages of "What a Great Question!", you've embarked on a transformative journey of self-discovery, growth, and leadership.

Through introspection, thoughtful reflection, and the power of inquiry, you've explored the depths of your inner world and uncovered the pathways to your greatest potential.

You've honed your communication skills, deepened your relationships, set meaningful goals, embraced feedback as a source of strength, and embarked on a journey of leadership and influence.

As you close this chapter of your life with this book, remember that your journey of self-improvement and leadership is an ongoing, never-ending story.

The questions you've encountered here are not the destination but rather the guiding stars that illuminate your path. They are the tools you carry with you as you venture into the unknown, facing challenges and seizing opportunities.

In your quest for personal and professional excellence, always remember that you have the power to shape your destiny, to inspire those around you, and to leave a legacy that transcends time.

Your leadership journey is a beacon of hope, a source of inspiration, and a testament to the human capacity for growth and positive change.

As you step forward, carry with you the lessons learned within these pages. Embrace the wisdom gained from self-discovery, the strength found in authentic communication, the clarity born of intentional goal-setting, the resilience nurtured through feedback, and the impact of ethical leadership. Share these lessons with others, for leadership is not a solitary pursuit but a collective effort to create a better world.

You are now equipped with the tools, the knowledge, and the vision to become the leader you aspire to be. Embrace the challenges, celebrate the successes, and continue to ask great questions.

Your journey is boundless, and your potential limitless. With each step, you contribute to the tapestry of leadership that shapes our world, leaving an indelible mark of inspiration, empowerment, and lasting change.

Thank you for allowing "What a Great Question" to be a part of your journey. Now, go forth and lead with purpose, compassion, and the unwavering belief in the power of questions to transform lives and create a brighter future.

The world awaits your leadership, and your legacy is yet to be written.

Dream big, ask boldly, and lead with heart.

Take time to reflect,

Work with Terry-Lyn

I offer a boutique consulting service for businesses and individuals looking to advance their people, performance and workplace culture.

Since 2002 I've come alongside corporates and SMEs to grow leadership capabilities and thriving cultures. My approach is simple, customised and real. I provide facilitation, training and coaching programs that make a genuine difference.

Your people will be empowered to lead effectively, authentically and with influence; your workplace will flourish with high-performing teams that drive the right outcomes.

I also work with individuals experiencing personal transition and seeking self-improvement; my 1:1 coaching programs are tailored to individual needs. I'm dedicated to seeing you and your business grow in a healthy, vigorous way.

www.terry-lyn.com.au

9 7 9 8 8 9 2 6 9 1 2 2 2